a gift for

from

PATSY CLAIRMONT

Pillow Prayers

to ease your mind

NASHVILLE, TENNESSEE

Published by the J. Countryman® division of the Thomas Nelson
Book Group., Nashville, Tennessee 37214

J. Countryman® is a trademark of Thomas Nelson, Inc.

The New King James Version (NKJV) ©1979, 1980, 1982, 1992,
Thomas Nelson, Inc., Publisher. Used by permission.

New Century Version® (NCV). Copyright © 1987, 1988, 1991 by
Thomas Nelson, Inc. All rights reserved. Used by permission.

The New American Bible (NAB) © 1987 by Thomas Nelson, Inc.
Used by permission.

Design: The DesignWorks Group; cover, John Hamilton;
        interior, Robin Black, www.thedesignworksgroup.com

Bedding photos in cooperation with Compleat Bed & Breakfast,
Bend, Oregon.

ISBN 1 4041 0178 0

Printed and bound in China

www.thomasnelson.com | www.jcountryman.com
www.womenoffaith.com

[Jesus] was . . .
asleep on a pillow.

MARK 4:38 NKJV

INTRODUCTION

I love the shadow-realm at the edge of sleep. It's usually so peaceful, a place where my mind drifts along the rivers of dreamland. But even better than that cozy haze is the sweet clarity of spending those precious moments with the Lord. He gives each day, and it's a joy to commune with Him at the very beginning and very end of them.

May the prayers and Scriptures in this little book guide you into sweeter rest in His arms and stronger rising in His love.

— *Patsy*

Rest in the LORD,
and wait patiently for Him;
PSALM 37:3 NKJV

The LORD has appeared of old to me, saying: "Yes, I have loved you with an everlasting love; Therefore with lovingkindness I have drawn you.

JEREMIAH 31:3 NKJV

oly Guard of the Night Watch, I relinquish myself to Your care. The day, crowded with demands, has wilted my strength. So, with gratitude, I lay my head upon my pillow.

Quiet my mind. Smooth from my brow the wrinkles that were knit by the concerns of the day.

Deliver me from rehashing that which, for now, cannot be altered. May Your comforting Spirit surround me with a sense of safety. In Your high intentions for me I find blessed relief.

God, who holds my yesterdays and who patrols my tomorrows, I trust in You tonight. Amen.

Morning Star, guide me through these daylight hours. Along my way, as I encounter people, may I do so with kindness. When I'm full of my plans, it's easy to think only of what matters to me. Deliver me from self-absorption. Even when others are insensitive, may I respond with gentle strength.

Today is full of opportunity to do good and to speak light-bearing words. When the hours collect into evening, may I look back over my offering and sense Your pleasure. I want to follow You and delight You all the days of my life. Amen.

The Lord GOD has given me a well-trained tongue, That I might know how to speak to the weary a word that will rouse them. Morning after morning he opens my ear that I may hear.

ISAIAH 50:4 NAB

In peace I shall both lie down and sleep,
for You alone, LORD, make me secure.

PSALM 4:8 NAB

*G*od over the Lonely Night, companion me. Your nearness causes my solitary struggle to ease. Your constancy steadies my pulse.

Twinges of regret threaten my calm, but release comes through Your mercy and forgiveness. Deliver me from the turmoil of surmising. Your invitation to lie down in peace woos me closer to the quiet stream. Like gentle waters washing over stones, trickle Your calm throughout my thoughts.

As I sleep, You remain steadfast at my side. My solace is in Your divine loyalty. Who but You has loved me this way? Amen.

unrise Song, thank You for the melody that stirs within me. My soul rejoices over Your goodness and Your continued generosity. You have taught my soul to sing and my feet to dance. Lord, I witness Your lavish heart toward Your own and respond with a sense of celebration, safety, and relief.

Teach me daily to make joyous sounds in Your presence and in the company of others. I want my life to have knee-slapping energy, and I desire my mouth to be full of Your praise. You alone are my song—my Divine Aria. I will sing of You. Amen.

I will sing of the mercies of the LORD forever; With my mouth will I make known Your faithfulness to all generations.

PSALM 89:1 NKJV

"I am the good shepherd. I know my sheep, as the Father knows me. And my sheep know me, as I know the Father. I give my life for the sheep."

JOHN 10:14 NCV

Shepherd of Eventide, gather me close to Your heart. Oversee my night. Still the restless inner voices of discontent that cause me to flail. Whisper goodwill into my spirit.

Thank You that in sleep we recover flagging energies. I pray You would purify my human longings, instill in me a deepening faith, and emblazon my hope.

In morning's first light may You find me committed to the tasks at hand, but for now I deliberately release my hold. In the protective safety of Your rod and staff I rest. I willingly enter the sheepfold of Your sovereign care. Amen.

orning Manna, I hunger for a word from You. I'm having trouble entering this day with joy. Pressures of work and the personalities of people have taxed my energy. Emotionally I feel edgy, mentally I feel scattered, and physically I feel worn.

To find afresh Your words and to gather them as a handmaiden filling her harvest basket brings me hope. Hope for new strength, balanced emotions, and single-mindedness.

May I taste and see that You are good. Feed me, Lord, that I might grow in grace toward others and rise up strong in You. Amen.

"I have heard the complaints of the children of Israel. Speak to them, saying, 'At twilight you shall eat meat, and in the morning you shall be filled with bread. And you shall know that I am the LORD your God.'"

EXODUS 16:12 NKJV

The voice of the LORD is over the waters;
the God of glory thunders, the LORD, over
the mighty waters. The voice of the LORD
is power; the voice of the LORD is splendor.

PSALM 29:3, 4 NAB

*S*tar-maker of a million lights pressed into the night, thank You for glimmers of hope. I'm easily lost without a lit path. Even in the fiercest storms You illuminate with swaths of lightning bolts against the angry sky.

I cozy my mind into my pillow and consider Your handiwork. It takes my breath away. Your dominance over darkness and Your presence in spite of it rally my heart. The rumble of thunder in the heavens reminds me of Your fierce power—power to handle the entire universe, much less my personal tempests while I sleep.

I rest in confidence. Amen.

Holy Helper, I'm in need of Your assistance. Today I'll have to make many decisions. Life is risky, and that scares me. Yet I'm aware that You redeem our mistakes. Knowing that's the case should take some of the threat out of my choices . . . yet I waiver.

Wouldn't it be easier to send me a telegram? Then I wouldn't bog down in the complications of my errors.

Is this unknown path part of faith? Is failure an important instructor? Is success my friend? Is humility birthed in mistakes or in obedience?

You who know and offer to guide my path, I take Your hand. Amen.

The LORD says, "I will make you wise and show you where to go. I will guide you and watch over you."

PSALM 32:8 NCV

So we do not give up. Our physical body is becoming older and weaker, but our spirit inside us is made new every day.

2 CORINTHIANS 4:16 NCV

*H*oly Healer, I know pain is a teacher, but do we need such a severe instructor? Are our loved ones, by their suffering, paying the price for our deepened compassion? Do we grab hold of grace . . . or does grace grab hold of us? Is there a moment in suffering when angels are dispatched?

I heard the flutter of wings tonight, hospice nurses gently assisting my loved one through the shadowed valley. Tenderly they turned her frail form and stroked her withered hand.

Strengthen me for my shifts in the valley until I come home. Amen.

Alpha, today is a new beginning. This page of my life is still clean. Help me not to scribble meaninglessly all over such a precious gift. Time has a way of skittering until sunset catches me unaware. I want to fully grasp my moments, whether in ease or in productivity; one restores, the other affirms.

I had thought some days had slipped through my fingers, but then I realized it was months, and now I know it was years. I can't retrieve those, but with Your empowerment I can embrace the rest of my beginnings with holy passion. May it be so. Amen.

The One on the throne said to me, "It is finished. I am the Alpha and the Omega, the Beginning and the End. I will give free water from the spring of the water of life to anyone who is thirsty."

REVELATION 21:6 NCV

Create in me a clean heart, O God,
And renew a steadfast spirit within me.

PSALM 51:10 NKJV

Champion of the Weary, thank You for undergirding my fragile being. I ache with exhaustion. Oh, Lord, help my whirring mind to settle into the quiet night.

You have brought me through another day. Align my heart with Your will. Rinse Your Spirit over impure and unkind thoughts that have found harbor within me. Kindly alert me if I have leaned into sin, lest I stumble down an unseemly way. Set my desires on elevated paths. Give me tenacity for Your higher plans.

I sink into my bed and, more importantly, into Your reassuring arms. Sleep comes as a friend. Amen.

Breath at Daybreak, resuscitate my courage to enter the demand-strewn path ahead. Help me not to pick up problems before they materialize. When I hit a dead end, help me not to camp out there. When I encounter a difficult person, help me not to join their fraternity. And when I am that person, remind me what it cost You for my freedom and forgiveness.

Breathe on me that I might rise up righteous from having been in Your presence. Earth needs more of heaven . . . as do I. Help me choose to walk in Your high counsel. Amen.

He gives to all life, breath, and all things.

ACTS 17:25 NKJV

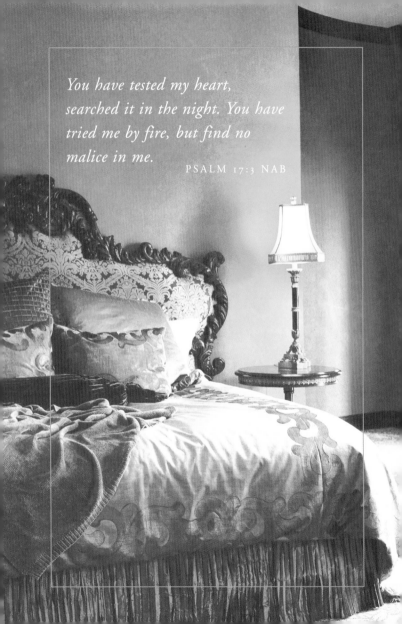

*You have tested my heart,
searched it in the night. You have
tried me by fire, but find no
malice in me.*   PSALM 17:3 NAB

V oice in the Stillness, speak to my listening heart. I wait, anticipating a divine exchange. Your voice calms my fears. Your visitations renew my peace. Your counsel clarifies my identity. Your guidance orders my daily steps.

One word from You and the lamb in me roars with newfound courage, courage that dissolves timidity and courage that nudges me to release others into Your tender guardianship. Supervise my loved ones' comings and goings. Tenderly make Yourself known to them.

Whisper holiness into my heart for all of our sakes. Your promises, O Lord, cause me to sleep deeply and well. Amen.

King Jesus, reign over my indignation. I must confront an enemy today. Truth can be treacherous and feel lethal. It's not my desire to inflict additional wounds but to walk in the light. Teach me to attack the problem and not the person.

You said, "There would be wars and rumors of wars" until Your return. So why am I stunned when someone wages war against me? Didn't I believe You?

Left on my own I might turn a simple skirmish into doomsday. I kneel before You and ask that You equip me for this encounter. Amen.

*Now to the King eternal, immortal,
invisible, to God who alone is wise,
be honor and glory forever and ever. Amen.*

1 TIMOTHY 1:17 NKJV

Like a shepherd he feeds his flock; in his arms he gathers the lambs, Carrying them in his bosom, and leading the ewes with care.

ISAIAH 40:11 NAB

Tender Lord Jesus, in the midst of
sorrow, my heart has turned into melted
wax. Without Your strength to give courage,
I cannot stand; without Your light to guide
through this ebony hour, I cannot wick; without
Your grace, my hope would be extinguished.

Upon those whom I love, pour out mercy
like anointing oil. Lift the weighty hours from
our minds and untie the tension that knots
deep within. Release Your cross-filled liberty
into our hearts.

You who goes before us, who steadies us
through the valley, who brings up the rear-
guard, announce Your strong presence among
us. Amen.

Day Glory, even before my eyes open I'm aware of birds singing outside my window. I hear the rustle of the curtains as the lace skims the sill. I feel the warmth of sunrays upon my hair. I'm aware of lilacs' perfume and leaves' gentle rustle. The gifts of nature calm me.

I ache to linger in this place between heaven and earth . . . but that is not what You have called me to. Lord, give me a new song, fragrance, and compassionate warmth to take through this day. And help me to bloom with calm. Amen.

He put a new song in my mouth, a song of praise to our God. Many people will see this and worship him. Then they will trust the Lord.

PSALM 40:3 NCV

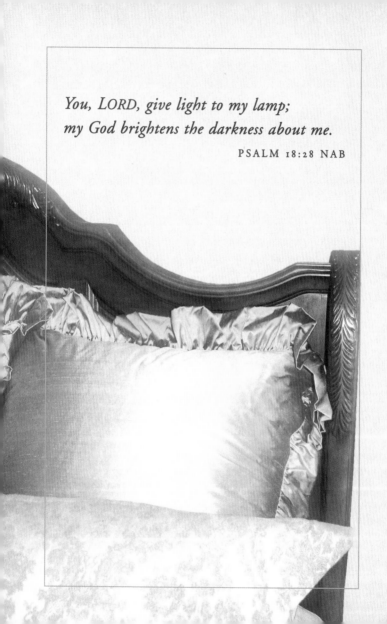

You, LORD, give light to my lamp;
my God brightens the darkness about me.

PSALM 18:28 NAB

*G*od Who Sees, enter my night. I'm grateful that Your view is not obstructed by darkness. I await Your intervention for my shadowed existence. Liberate me from myopic tendencies lest I live out my life in a restricted space.

Some days my opinions block out healing truth. My dingy motives can slip past me unrecognized. Release me from the entanglement of sight-altering distractions—inconveniences, interruptions, and other people's behavior.

The horizon brightens as I focus on You. Light the landscape of my life with Your presence. I long to live out my days in Your radiance. Amen.

Heart's Joy, fill me with a sense of Your constancy. For me, Your love is like a handful of kite strings in the fragile grip of a child—hard to hold onto. Yet when I become tangled in branches of bitterness and powerlines of anger, I feel Your tugs of conviction working to nudge me free.

Your acceptance of me buoys my existence, and Your forgiveness causes me to soar. Thank You for not giving up on me. Thank You for not leaving me entwined in my calamity. Thank You for holding me fast. You are my daily joy. Amen.

Jesus Christ is the same yesterday, today, and forever.

HEBREWS 13:8 NKJV

The LORD is my shepherd; I shall not want.
He makes me to lie down in green pastures;
He leads me beside the still waters.
He restores my soul; He leads me in the paths
of righteousness For His name's sake.
Surely goodness and mercy shall follow me
All the days of my life; And I will
dwell in the house of the LORD Forever.

PSALM 23:1-3,6 NKJV

Gentle Shepherd, help me to breathe serenity deep into my valley life. Guide me to places of refreshment. Release me from the intimidation of rocky paths. Help my eyes to adjust to the lighted way. Prepare my feet for craggy terrain. Lead me to Your high places.

Allow the oil of Your Spirit to soften any resistance within me. Unwind my tangled thoughts and calm my tattered emotions.

May I lavish Your provisions on others.

Your compassion is my pillow and Your mercies my coverlet. May Your goodness flourish within me. And may my heart remain faithful all the days of my life. Amen.

Holy One, enter my heart's sanctuary. Purify my intentions. Inspect my thoughts. Create an acceptable place within me for Your Spirit to dwell.

Smudges of greed, jealousy, and envy stain the altar of my soul. I wrestle with neediness and insecurity. Forgive me. Cleanse me. Heal me. Claim Your rightful place. Enthrone my heart.

Revise my agenda. Infuse my mission. Empower my efforts. Beacon my path.

Instruct me in adoration, supplication, and celebration. You and You only are worthy of high honor and continual praise. I commit to serve You all of my days. Amen.

Search me, O God, and know my heart;
Try me, and know my anxieties;
And see if there is any wicked way in me,
And lead me in the way everlasting.

PSALM 139:23, 24 NKJV

*Happy the people who know you,
LORD, who walk in the radiance
of your face.*

PSALM 89:15 NAB

Guiding Light, for the first time today, as evening enfolds me, I'm still. Movement keeps adversaries at bay, but I know I must rest. Enemies seem more threatening in the night. My problems rise up and cast Goliath-sized shadows across my pebble-sized faith.

Darkness is dispelled in Your presence, and one day, night will be noonday bright. You know until then I need lights to hearten me—the light of Your presence, Your path, and Your peace.

As I brighten my thoughts with Your promises, it's as if I've found a slingshot for my pebble. Amen.

Word of Life, advise me. My thoughts can spark words that cause harm; I know that was not Your intention. Instead, may I speak life-giving words. Help me to proclaim Your liberty to fear-bound captives. I want the wounded to find shelter in my conversation with them.

Thank You for those along life's journey who have spoken kindly to me. Who have uttered words fit and wise. They have shared Your love and counsel. They have generously affirmed the gifts You placed within me that I had not recognized. I want to do that for others. Regenerate my vocabulary; permeate it with vitality. Amen.

*Like golden apples in silver settings are
words spoken at the proper time.*

PROVERBS 25:11 NAB

Finally, brothers, whatever is true, whatever is honorable, whatever is just, whatever is pure, whatever is lovely, whatever is gracious, if there is any excellence and if there is anything worthy of praise, think about these things.

PHILIPPIANS 4:8 NAB

*M*atchless Illuminator, bring Your holy lantern into the corridors of my mind. Speak Your longings into my thoughts. Turn me away from my gloomy musings. Usher me into the safety of Your meditations. Deliver me from small speculations. Fix my thoughts on Your expansive agenda.

Spark my mind with vitality. Breathe Your purity into the unlit corners of my imagination. Ignite Your purposes within me.

As I think on You, I'm aware that You first thought of me. The magnetism of that understanding draws me back to You again and again. I fall asleep comforted by Your pursuing love. Amen.

Living Well, I thirst. My soul is arid. The unrelenting winds of hardship have left me parched. My mind wanders from one mirage to another until I remember that You quench my thirst.

Your Word becomes mercy drops to my brittle bones. Your voice is morning dew. A sense of Your presence is summer rain. Settle on me like a well-watered garden that Your reign might cause me to grow again.

Meditating on You causes a stream to run through my desert heart. I kneel and drink, that I might rise and follow. Replenish worthy desires in me. Amen.

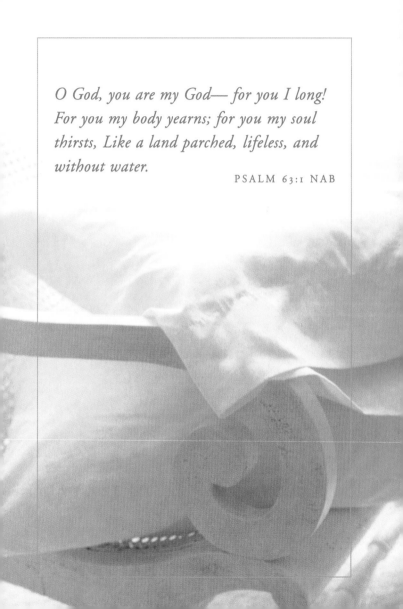

O God, you are my God— for you I long!
For you my body yearns; for you my soul
thirsts, Like a land parched, lifeless, and
without water.

PSALM 63:1 NAB

Jesus answered and said to him, "If anyone loves Me, he will keep My word; and My Father will love him, and We will come to him and make Our home with him.

*W*insome Savior, I'm grateful for Your continual presence. I implore You this evening to scour my heart of spite and cruelty and to adorn me in Your many graces. Untie the gnawing tension in my stomach, shoulders, jaw, and aching back. Liberate me from the strain of self-assertion that I might acquiesce to Your higher plans.

Quiet my pounding heart, my pressing fears, and my personal agendas. Nurture my wilted soul, soften my severe features, and add luster to my dull eyes.

I pray Your stunning beauty would be seen in my repose, rhetoric, and responses. Amen.

Promise Keeper, did You mean it when You said, "Love your enemies"? Because I'm struggling to love even those I genuinely care for. I justify my emotional limitations on their behavior, but I know better. My responses are my daily business before You.

Reveal my inconsistencies, that I might experience greater wholeness. Expose my narrowness, that I might experience Your fullness. Divulge my secrets, that I might experience Your emancipation.

Help me to grow a wide love and a deep character. And remind me that blame is not a worthy game.

Thank You for keeping Your promises— help me to keep mine. Amen.

Get along with each other, and forgive each other. If someone does wrong to you, forgive that person because the Lord forgave you.

COLOSSIANS 3:13 NCV

Yes, in joy you shall depart, in peace you shall be brought back; Mountains and hills shall break out in song before you, and all the trees of the countryside shall clap their hands.

ISAIAH 55:12 NAB

*P*eacekeeper, I confess that today I ran slipshod through my hours, forgetting Your offer of a way less traveled, a steadfast path, untroubled waters, and safe resting places. Thank You that I can find protection from my hurriedness in Your care.

Massage my heart with Your calming spirit that I might be renewed in strength. Because of You, tomorrow holds the promise of a quiet heart. I surrender to Your keeping grace.

Tonight in Your consoling presence, harmonious rhythms replace my frenzy.

Thank You for evening closure . . . Sleep, sweet sleep arrives as a welcomed friend. Amen.

Heaven's Glory, I witness the declaration of Your presence above me: Pillow-tufted clouds. Scattered sunrays falling on garden floors. Winds, fluttering flags, ringing chimes, lifting kites. Endless blue skies canopying the earth.

Your handiwork shouts, sings, and whispers to us of Your divine fingerprints, holy kisses, and sacred embraces. When I am warmed by the sun, cooled by a breeze, and refreshed by Your hue-strewn artistry, I am reminded that You prepared all this for us.

I enter this day with joyful gratitude. Thank You for the wonders of creation and the glorious pleasure of Your company. Amen.

The heavens declare the glory of God;
the sky proclaims its builder's craft.

PSALM 19:1 NAB

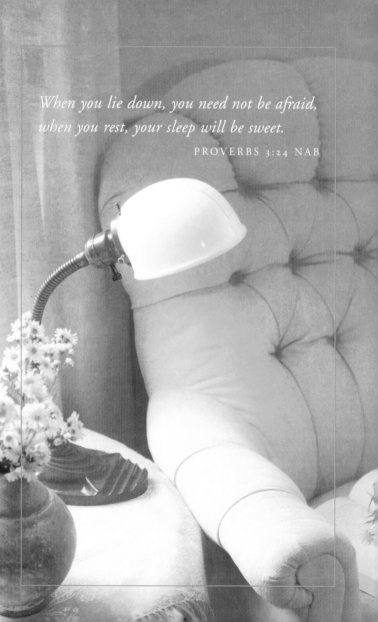

When you lie down, you need not be afraid,
when you rest, your sleep will be sweet.

PROVERBS 3:24 NAB

*S*leep-Giver, rest flickers within me. Worries scamper about my room like mice in a pantry. Footfalls of fear stomp down the halls of my mind.

And then I remember Your . . .

Sheltering love. Comforting mercies. River peace. Holy counsel. Forgiving grace. Eternal kindness. Brimming joy. Forever presence.

Oh, Spirit of God, enthrone my heart anew. Steady my concerns. Lamplight my struggles with Your clear counsel. Calm me with a fresh realization of the security I have in You.

I lay my head down on my pillow and await sleep's overtaking release . . . and if it hesitates, I will settle my thoughts on You. Amen.

riend of Sinners, forgive my self-serving ways. Teach me how to take care of myself without my exacting unnecessary payment from others. Teach me servanthood without my turning it into martyrdom. Teach me success without my allowing it to inflate my ego.

Thank You, Jesus, for not shunning me for my ragged righteousness. Or abandoning me when my walk teeters. Or forsaking me when I fail miserably.

You truly love completely. In You I find companionship, forgiveness, acceptance, privilege, discipline, and safety. I'm thankful for Your sandal-clad heart that keeps You close. What an honor to call You *Friend.* Amen.

*Have mercy on me, God, in Your goodness;
in Your abundant compassion blot out
my offense.*

PSALM 51:1 NAB

He will be your safety. He is full of salvation, wisdom, and knowledge. Respect for the Lord is the greatest treasure.

ISAIAH 33:6 NCV

ight Architect, examine my heart's orbit. Sometimes I live by rote and lose sight of Your spectacular ways. The stir of the Spirit helps to bring me back around to You and to the constellation of Your purposes. In Your divine placement I find meaning and direction.

I've noted that as I pray, my apathy subsides, opinions dissipate, and confusion clears. Your love enlivens my emotions. Your nearness centers my world.

You who cradled the moon, ignited the stars, set the path of the planets, and wrapped us in the blanket of nightfall, I rest in Your wondrous design. Amen.

Merciful Messenger, deliver me from the wasteland of excuses. I long to leave a rich history, footprints for others to follow. Yet I'm often guilty of idleness. Spark fervor within me so those who come after me will find a clear path to You.

Speak life into any barren agendas I have, that they might bring forth pleasing fruit. I realize I can do the right thing for the wrong reasons. Purify my infected motives. Cleanse me of calculated kindnesses. Instruct me in integrity.

I'm listening for Your merciful voice, tender or stern. Enable me to sprint toward truth. Amen.

Keep me from the sins of pride;
don't let them rule me.
Then I can be pure and
innocent of the greatest
of sins.

PSALM 19:13 NCV

Be renewed in the spirit of your mind.

EPHESIANS 4:23 NKJV

Friend of Sinners, I'm pacing. Harsh words spoken by another keep replaying inside me. Help me not to obsessively rifle through the conversation in search of more than was there. Protect me from coddling pride as if it's my best friend. Instead, cause me to hold fast to grace. Remind me again, Lord Jesus, what You paid for my harshness that I might know Your liberty.

I'm quick to cry "judgment" when I'm offended and "mercy" when I offend. Help me to release my offender through forgiveness, like You did for us all before we were even sorry. Amen.

*W*ay Maker, this morning started off like a crooked path. Things were not going the way I had hoped. Irritations rubbed against my emotions like grit in a sandal. It's taken years, but You've taught me that I—and others—do not need to be victims of my moods. You have taught me to gird up my mind, cast down imaginations, choose truth, and stand fast.

It's a relief to get over myself and on with the day, focused on the way I should go. Keep me on the straight and narrow path, that I might experience the width and depth of Your provisions. Amen.

Thus says the LORD, your redeemer, the Holy One of Israel: I, the LORD, your God, teach you what is for your good, and lead you on the way you should go.

ISAIAH 48:17 NAB

I find rest in God; only he gives me hope.

PSALM 62:5 NCV

Holy Renewer, I've pushed toward deadlines and other people's expectations. Now I'm spent. I don't regret an active life unless my efforts divert me from Your superior path. My desire is that my energies bring forth enduring results.

Past seasons of inactivity have left me guilt-ridden; so I find my exhaustion satisfying . . . yet I realize that in my attempts to be vital I can dash right past Your best.

In this whirlwind world give me eyes to see Your high calling, ears to hear Your wooing voice, and restraint to keep me from careening off Your path. Amen.

ock of Ages, I need a solid place to stand. This tilt-a-whirl world makes me wobbly. Disasters, floods, wars, and terrorists spread like plagues throughout the land. Headlines tout insurrection of Your ways. Values thin. Apathy breeds. Negligence abounds.

Waken my sensibilities to Your high calling. Cause me to rise out of apathy's ashes and rejoin the race. Move me past my insecurities. Use my voice for good. Give me vision to see beyond the enemy's foils.

Though the world shake, may I stand firm in You. "On Christ the solid rock I stand, all other ground is sinking sand." Amen.

I keep the LORD before me always. Because he is close by my side, I will not be hurt.

PSALM 16:8 NCV

This is what the LORD says: "Stand where the roads cross and look. Ask where the old way is, where the good way is, and walk on it. If you do, you will find rest for yourselves."

JEREMIAH 6:16 NCV

Heavenly Restorer, I wrestle with my thoughts. Why is it that my mind swirls while my body aches for sleep? Old voices of reproach and guilt nag. Lord, You paid for forgiveness and You extend grace, so why do I allow past failures to bully me?

I sometimes forget my capacity for self-absorption, which leads to indulgent pity. Free me from destructive thoughts.

Cleansing goodness and heart-healing kindness fill Your plans. You call me to walk uprightly, that I might be strengthened in personal integrity. Your instructions protect me from the thickets of regret.

Return me to the ancient path. Amen.

Day Brightener, I awakened at dawn as the morning sun dappled my pillow. Thank You for the reassurance You have pressed into creation that affirms Your presence and overriding care. Today is packed full of responsibility, but for now I bask in the quietness of these refreshing moments.

Later, when I am knee-deep in my day, may I stop and reflect long enough to allow Your calm to influence my frenetic schedule. My busyness can cause me to place more importance on achievements than relationships. Help me to balance my activities with a heart-felt interest in others. Light my way. Amen.

LORD, every morning you hear my voice.
Every morning, I tell you what I need, and I
wait for your answer.

PSALM 5:3 NCV

I will bless the LORD who has given me counsel; My heart also instructs me in the night seasons.

PSALM 16:7 NKJV

onderful Counselor, speak Your words into my spirit. Loose me from my shallow routines. I keep falling headlong into the pit of habit. I want to change, but I need a Samaritan's hand to pull me out of this familiar pit.

Perhaps I need a holy jolt.

Yet . . . be gentle, for I have found that truth, like thunderbolts, is full of both light and fury. I'm too weary for fury. Would You counsel me in the night hours? Then I'll awake refreshed and braver.

I believe You desire our lives to brim over with purposeful meaning. I await Your counsel. Amen.

O mega, I'm relieved that You have the final say . . . in life, work, relationships, politics, wars, and death. Not that I don't question Your ways and Your timing, but You knew we wouldn't fully understand Your divine agenda. What brings me comfort and peace is realizing that, even when I don't "get it," I can trust Your loving heart and Your perfect plan.

If there were no plan in place, no sovereign hand to lead, we would live without purpose, having no resources beyond ourselves, and left to the whim of every wind. I take refuge in Your finality. Amen. ❧

But the plan of the LORD stands forever,
wise designs through all generations.

PSALM 33:11 NAB

There is a place of quiet rest,
Near to the heart of God,
A place where sin cannot molest,
Near to the heart of God.
There is a place of full release,
Near to the heart of God,
A place where all is joy and peace,
Near to the heart of God.

—CLELAND B. MCAFEE, 1901

He gives His beloved sleep.

PSALM 127:2 NKJV

I will lift up my eyes to the hills—From whence
    comes my help?
My help comes from the LORD,
Who made heaven and earth.
He will not allow your foot to be moved;
He who keeps you will not slumber.
Behold, He who keeps Israel
Shall neither slumber nor sleep.
The LORD is your keeper;
The LORD is your shade at your right hand.
The sun shall not strike you by day,
Nor the moon by night.
The LORD shall preserve you from all evil;
He shall preserve your soul.
The LORD shall preserve your going out and your
    coming in
From this time forth, and even forevermore.

PSALM 121 NKJV

*Return to your rest, O my soul,
For the LORD has dealt bountifully
with you.*

PSALM 116:7 NKJV